I0505610

# Table Of Contents (TOC)

# Introduction

Thank you and I honestly congratulate you for downloading the book "**How to start a business from home: 10 online income streams that will generate consistent passive income each month**"

In this book you will find:

- Why you should work from home
- Why you should start a business from home
- How you can generate passive money
- 10 different proven methods which can bring you thousands of dollars
- Different ways to combine the income streams between them
- Illustrations and images which show how the income streams work

# Chapter 1: Why Should You Work From Home?

Why should you work full time every day for a company or for a boss who doesn't pay you enough or doesn't care about you?

Why should you go to work each day at 8:00 AM and feel tired all day and stressed out?

I know, nobody likes that, and the good news is that what internet offers today and how the world has evolved in the past few years, it now offers you great opportunities. Opportunities like freelancing, creating a small company from home, creating an online company, website, blog, channel etc.

There are a lot of ways to make money online, a lot of people have succeeded in generating passive income, month after month, and the best part about this is that you can constantly grow and expand, your work will remain there, for a long period of time.

What benefits do you get by working from home?

I'm glad you've asked. Here are the major benefits of staying home and working:

1. Flexible schedule – even if you have to manage your time to achieve your goals and to finish what you start. You wake up when you want, you work how much you want and you can have how many free days you want. You are your own boss.

2. More time – imagine yourself working when you travel by train from Paris to Amsterdam or from LA to New York on an airplane or being everywhere in this world, you just check your emails, money and stats.
3. Less stress – nobody tells you what to do, you make your research, you do your work, you can have a break whenever you want without getting noticed by your boss what to do.
4. Fast growth – if you work full time for a company, you will grow, you will get higher wages if you work hard and efficient, but your salary raise will be in a matter of months or even years.
5. You invest in yourself – you achieve knowledge and you apply them for your personal business, not for somebody else.
6. You can hire other people easily – you can hire people to do simple tasks or long time tasks in order to grow your income and business. And the best part is that you can hire freelancers inexpensively, without contracts and without much effort – it's simple, you hire the best people you find and the ones who work hard and efficient.

The list can go on, there are dozens of benefits.

# Chapter 2: Multiple Online Income Streams

Now, here comes the most interesting fact of the book – how can you generate money online and work from home. Here are 10 of the most powerful online income streams. Now I am just enouncing the income streams and then I will present in detail each of them.

1. Amazon Kindle (KDP) – you can generate thousands of dollars just by publishing eBooks, you can write your own eBooks, about any topic, money, self-development, cookbooks, science, fiction stories, diseases etc. (just search a few topics on Kindle to see what I'm talking about)
2. Affiliate marketing – advertise and market somebody else's products on the web, on your YouTube channel, on your Facebook, on your website, on your blog etc.

3. Make online courses – Udemy and Clickbank – on these websites you can create your own digital products and courses about anything – you can create coaching courses, about different topics, if you know a software (such as Adobe Photoshop) or how to make money online, or how to use a program etc. ; you can make a course of 2-3 hours or even more and people will buy it if it's good.
4. Write articles/ebooks – iWriter – if you like to write, to create original content and you can do that fast, you can earn a lot of money – people are constantly looking for writers.
5. Web Design – 99designs.com – if you have advanced knowledge about Adobe Photoshop for example, you can design websites and earn hundreds even thousands of dollars just from a design. (it has to be high quality though)
6. Work as a virtual assistant – this is the easiest and fastest way to earn money online, every busy business man needs his stuff to be done quickly. You will earn hundreds of dollars from this.
7. Work as a photographer – take beautiful shots and upload them on fotolia.com, shutterstock.com or istockphoto.com. A lot of companies need professional licensed photos to use for their projects. You can earn thousands here too.
8. Work as a 3D Designer – Turbosquid.com – design 3D models in Autodesk 3Ds Max, Autodesk Maya, ZBrush and upload them on turbosquid.com – the biggest 3D online market. By uploading models there, they will remain there and you will get passive income while you are working for your next projects.
9. Create websites – make different websites on different niches and put affiliate links or adds from

Google (Google AdSense) – the more traffic you get on your website, the more money you will make.

10. YouTube – make a series of videos on a certain topic (niche), make a show, a video each week or something similar, the possibilities are infinite here. The more videos you have, the more views you get, the more money you receive back.

# Chapter 3: EBooks

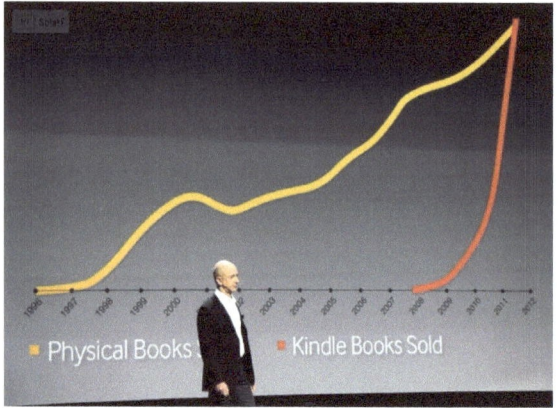

EBooks are now more and more popular, people will stop buying paperback books and it's natural to be so – imagine that now everybody has smartphones, laptops, tablets and other smart gadgets. (Smarwatches, soon Smartglasses – check out Google Glass)

The advantages of eBooks over paperback books:

- A lot faster to deliver (less than 30 seconds for Amazon to deliver your book wirelessly on your device)
- Cheaper – digital – no paper, no ink, no additional costs, no transport
- You can have an almost unlimited number (an eBook has in average about 0.5 – 2 MB)
- You can carry an unlimited number of books with you on your account – on one tablet you can have for

example 1000 eBooks. How would you carry 1000 physical books with you all the time?

- Environmental friendly – you do not have to cut any trees in order to make paper to get your book. It's digital, 100% eco.

In other words, people are buying more and more books and this market is constantly growing, each year the number of eBooks is growing and more and more people are looking forward to buying eBooks rather than paperback books.

Independently publish with Kindle Direct Publishing to reach millions of readers

**Get to market fast.** Publishing takes less than 5 minutes and your book appears on Kindle stores worldwide within 24-48 hours.

**Make more money.** Earn up to 70% royalty on sales to customers in the US, Canada, UK, Germany, India, France, Italy, Spain, Japan, Brazil, Mexico, Australia and more. Enroll in KDP Select and earn more money through Kindle Unlimited and the Kindle Owners' Lending Library.

**Keep control.** Keep control of your rights and set your own list prices. Make changes to your books at any time.

**Get started today!** Publish your books with KDP. Learn how to get started.

You can earn more than 10,000$ / month with Amazon KDP by publishing all kinds of books: cookbooks, health books, development books, science books, fiction books, erotica books, professional books, language books, biographies, children's books, illustrations etc.

You can write down on any niche that you want. Just write a good quality book and people will start to buy it. It's a short process to follow – choose a niche, write your book, format it (write it in Microsoft Word or Pages for Mac), order or design a cover – you can order an inexpensive cover on www.Fiverr.com for 5 – 10$ or you can order a 100% professional cover on www.99designs.com but it will be at least 299$. When you have your cover and your book ready – upload the book in a few steps on www.kdp.amazon.com and your book is available for purchase worldwide.

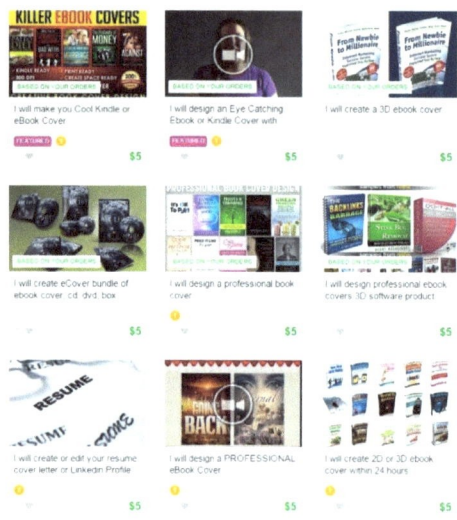

Repeat this process and make a bigger number of books.

Here's a fact – you do not have to be a good writer – you can write your own nonfiction books (even fiction books if you have some imagination) or you can hire other people to do that for you. You just order some articles, chapters on www.Freelancer.com or on www.iWriter.com, you proof read your book (on Fiverr as well if you want, for 5-10$), you edit it and you are ready to go.

In order to make money on Amazon KDP you will have to price your books between 2.99$ and 9.99$ to get the 70% royalty. If the book's price is outside this range, you will get 0.35% and you don't want that. After all, a 2.99$ price is inexpensive, especially for books between 30 and 100 pages.

A good book will generate you, in average, between 50 and 200$ / month (including borrows, you get paid for borrows as well). If you create 5 books in a month you will get 250 – 1000$ in the next month. Imagine if you create 100 books in 1 year, you will generate at least 5000$ / month.

The process is easy, from start to finish, the fact is that you will have to promote your books in order to get some sales, Amazon has a lot of promotional tools to promote your books at the beginning 5 days every 90 days – KDP Select program.

The best part is that once your book is promoted and set up, it will bring you money constantly, each month, for years, without doing any additional tasks or costs.

If you do not want to publish your eBooks on Amazon Kindle you can publish them on www.smashwords.com or on www.barnesandnoble.com

In what place can you work 1 year constantly and then to receive a few thousands of dollars each month, even while you sleep?

# Chapter 4: Affiliate Marketing

Affiliate marketing is one of the most popular and one of the most fastest ways to make money online by advertising somebody else's product on the web.

It's simple, somebody creates a product or sells a physical, even a digital product and you advertise that product. When somebody buys that product from your link (it's all about links), you get a commission (from 5 to even 50%, it depends).

Where can you search for affiliate products / Where can you get affiliate links from?

There a lot of platforms which offer an affiliate program, one of the biggest (in fact, the biggest) is Amazon Associates.

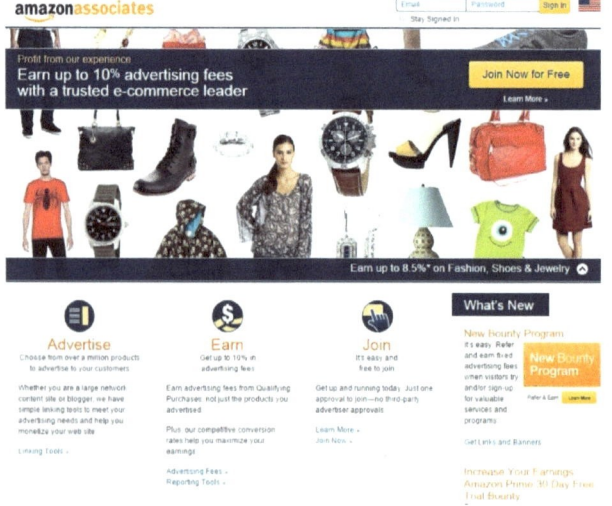

As soon as you sign up for Amazon's affiliate program, you can access thousands of products which you can advertise.

Amazon also gives you some tools to help you create an aStore – an Amazon based store with products which you can review and advertise. Then, by promoting that aStore, you will get traffic and of course people who will be interested in buying those products.

Here's a cool fact about these affiliate links – if you put an affiliate link for a laptop, I, as a buyer click on your link and look at the laptop, but I click on a related product from the suggestions and I buy a tablet, you will also get paid. In other words, everything you buy on Amazon through an affiliate link, you get a commission.

You don't have to use an aStore if you don't want to. You can make your own blog, your own website on a certain topic.

For example, you can make an Automotive website with car reviews, car accessories reviews and after you finish the article you can put the affiliate link – to purchase the product presented, click on the link below => affiliate link.

It's so simple.

You can even put the affiliate link anywhere – on your Facebook page, YouTube channel, on a Facebook Fan Page (recommended) or wherever you like. Anybody who buys from that link gets you a commission.

Example: you make an electronic aStore – smartphones, tablets, accessories, laptops. You have 200 products. You sell 3 laptops which costa 1000$ and the commission is 10%. You instantly make 3 x 10% x 1000$ = 300$ from 3 sales.

See how powerful this is?

Amazon isn't the only place from where you can get your affiliate links. You can put affiliate links from eBay for example.

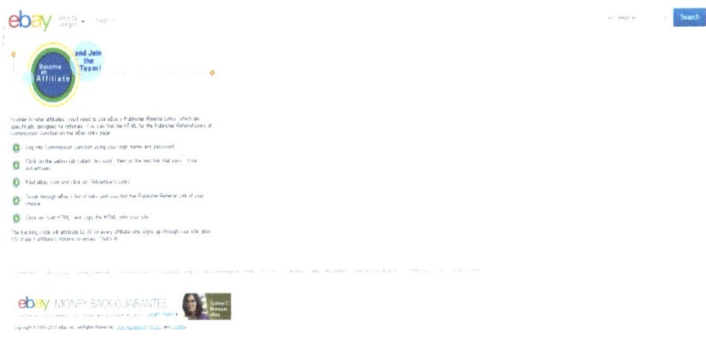

Now here's something you'll find interesting – you can advertise somebody else's products depending on what website, blog or what you are specialized in AND you can even create your own products, courses, digital products, physical products that others can sell for you and you will receive the money you want.

For example, you create a digital course of 3 hours which you want to sell online and it costs 99$. You give people a commission of 20% and a lot of advertisers will be interested in promoting your product.

If you were able to sell by yourself 100 copies a month and generate 10,000$, imagine how would it be to sell 500 copies but to earn only 80% from that product.

100 copies of your own = 10,000$ + 400 copies which other people advertised = 400 x 80$ = 32,000$

You will make 42,000$.

Maybe I've exaggerated a little bit with the numbers, but the important thing is for you to get the idea, you can triple or quadruple your earnings with the help of affiliate members.

The best place to put your product for others to advertise, if it's a digital product, is on ClickBank.

You'll find products to advertise or people to advertise your products. It's best to combine them. Make a website or a store with products you advertise and make your own digital product that others may advertise for you.

All in all, affiliate marketing is relatively easy to do and very profitable. It depends on the product you advertise and how you promote the products, it's a profitable passive income stream. You set up some links, you promote them and you're done. While you're asleep, money goes into your bank account. Isn't it sweet?

There are dozens of companies and websites and stores which have affiliate programs. Advertise what you like and what you are good at.

# Chapter 5: Create Digital Courses

This is a very profitable income stream from which you can generate a six figure annual passive income. The best places where you can sell your digital courses is on www.Udemy.com and on www.clickbank.com

On Udemy, there are courses which are free, and courses which are even more than 499$, it depends on the number of hours and the niche of the course.

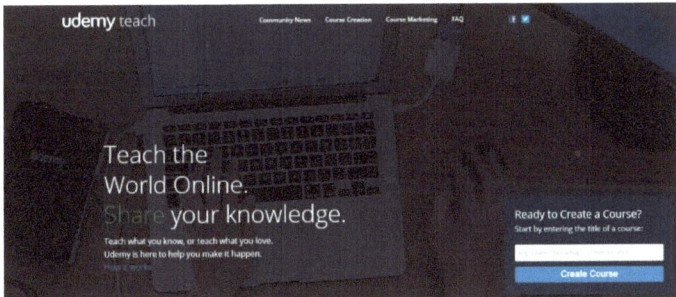

What kind of digital courses can you sell on Udemy?

You can make courses about "How to learn Photoshop", "How to learn Web Design", "How to manage your time effectively", generally know how products work well.

In order to create a course, you record the screen and talk. In other words, you make short and good quality tutorials – 2 minutes to 30 minutes even an hour, but I don't recommend to do that. Make 10 minute tutorials, for example 20 tutorials – 2 of 5 minutes – the intro and the finish and the other ones to have a 10 minute length.

The tutorials must be organized in sections (chapters) - make sure to have at least 20 tutorials of 5 – 10 minutes each and you will have 2-3 hours of content. People want to know how much time do they need to go through all the course.

You only need a good quality microphone and a screen recording software (such as Camtasia) and you can record the course from your laptop, from any place in this world. You put your knowledge on the screen and you talk about it. The voice has to be good quality, and the videos must be at least HD, recommended is to record Full HD.

You do not need to appear on screen, you just talk about yourself at the beginning, so people know who you are and then you go right into the main subject that you are presenting.

Make several courses, and passive money will come in your bank account each month. Make sure to advertise your courses, pay for that if it's necessary and you're done.

Udemy also has an affiliate program, so if you want others to promote your course, just sign up for that and you will get more students (that's how customers are called on Udemy).

What you are not allowed to do on Udemy is to put courses of yours which are also on YouTube for free. If you sell your course on Clickbank, it's ok, they don't mind that.

You can also sell your digital product on www.clickbank.com

You put your product there and people will advertise your product. You will get an additional passive income from that as well.

To make a 2 hour course, it will require about a week of work, if the course is a good quality course you can price it from 49$ to 99$ and if you promote it properly you can get more than 50 -100 students a month which means a lot of money.

Online courses are easy to access, inexpensive, you have lifetime access to them on your pc, tablets and smartphones.

# Chapter 6: Write Articles Or eBooks

If you're keen on writing and creating content and you want to get paid as soon as you finish your work, writing articles might fit you. All you need is imagination and a laptop.

What kind of articles can you write?

You can write about anything you want, you can focus only on certain topics and niches that you like or at which you are good at.

Where can you write?

You can write on www.freelancer.com people are looking for writers, ghostwriters, people who can write fiction stories or any kinds or articles.

You can receive for as low as 3$/article of 500 words up to 2000$ for a good fiction book of 100 pages. To earn that money on freelancer it requires some experience, so for the beginning you will get paid pretty low.

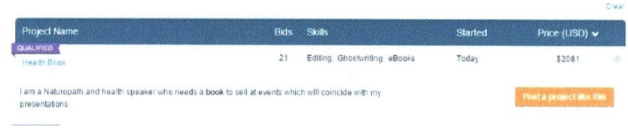

If you don't want to waste time or to lose projects by bidding on freelancer, you can go directly on www.iWriter.com and get to work as fast as possible. Prices vary there from 1.25$ / article of 150 words up to 110$ / article of 2000 words.

On iWriter, there are some levels for which you get paid differently:

1. Basic Writer (new writer) – you get 1.25$ / article of 150 words up to 14$/article of 2000 words
2. Premium Writer (minimum 30 article written and at least 4.1/5 star overall rating) – you get paid from 2.75$/article of 150 words up to 30$/article of 2000 words.
3. Elite Writer (minimum 40 articles written and at least 4.6/5 overall rating) – you get paid from 4.25$/article of 150 words up to 40$/article of 2000 words.
4. Elite Plus Writer (minimum 40 articles written and at least 4.85/5 overall rating) – you get paid from 10$/article of 150 words up to 110$/article of 2000 words.

* Basic      : All writers will see your request.
  Premium  : 4.1 to 5 star writers will see your request.
  Elite       : 4.6 to 5 star writers will see your request.
  Elite Plus : 4.85 to 5 star writers will see your request.

You can also write eBooks on iWriter – an eBook with 20 pages, formatted correctly is only for Premium, Elite and Elite Plus Writers and you get paid starting from 160$ for a 20 page book, up to 790$/ 100 page eBook. Elite Writers will earn between 210$ and 1050$ for an eBook between 20 and 100 pages (2,000 to 35,000 words) and Elite Plus Writers can earn from 580$ to 2890$ for an eBook which has between 20 and 100 pages.

**Submit a new project**

Fill out the information below to have content written by iWriters.
You can view a tutorial video on creating a project by clicking here.

| | |
|---|---|
| Project type | Have an eBook written |
| Project description | |
| Category | All |
| eBook length | 35 000 - 100 pages |
| Article language | English (US) |
| Submit to | Premium — 4.1 to 5 star writers will see your request<br>Elite — 4.6 to 5 star writers will see your request<br>• Elite Plus — 4.85 to 5 star writers will see your request |
| Load previous project data ▾ Project price | $0.00 (minimum $2890.00 per article) |
| Chapter titles | • You choose the titles for the writer<br>○ Allow writer to make up their own titles |

As you can see, writing articles can be a very profitable income stream – but this one isn't passive, it's an active one. What you do today, you will be paid today as well. If you work hard at the beginning, in a couple of months you will get a premium badge and you will be able to make more money.

An article of 500 words will be written if you have good writing skills in less than 1 hour an you will get around 6$ if you are a Premium Writer and up to 25$ if you are an Elite Plus Writer.

Here's a cool fact – if the person who requires the articles likes your work, he can tip you and also can add you to his favorite list of writers and can give you exclusive projects.

A writer who works everyday 3-4 hours a day, can earn +1000$/month as a part time job, from home, from your laptop, from anywhere. You have to be creative and to write good quality content.

# Chapter 7: Become A Web Designer

A lot of people are focusing on Adobe Photoshop, Logo design and especially on Web Design. It's a profitable way to make money and the best part is that you can make both active and passive money: you can make money actively by taking projects directly from customers around the world (300 – 3000$ / website) or passive - you can make themes and sell them per download (15 – 100$ / download).

Imagine that you can make 50 website theme (wordpress themes sell best) and you will easily make hundreds even thousands of dollars each month, passively. While you earn money passively you can also work on 1 on 1 projects actively.

You can sell/buy wordpress themes, PSD themes and other types of designs used for building websites on www.themeforest.net it is one of the largest markets out there, there are themes starting from 3$ and up to 100$ or even more, depending on the niche and the purpose of the website that you are building.

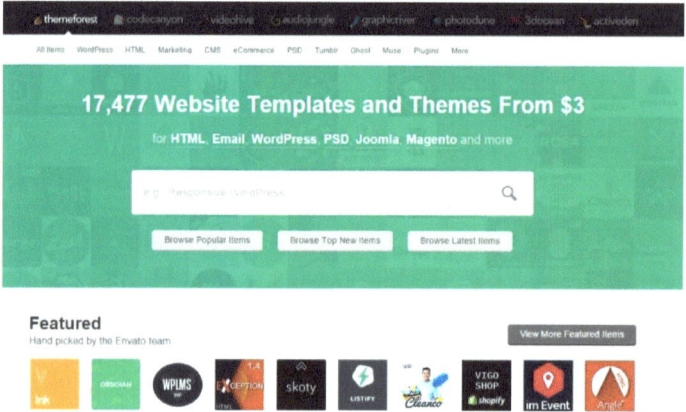

There are other websites as well, but this one is very popular.

To work on projects actively, the best place to make money is www.99designs.com or www.freelancer.com – you will find projects, contests and even jobs (on freelancer) and you can make thousands of dollars for each project.

On 99designs, you will compete with other designers in a contest and you will get ratings for everything you do. This is tricky, because you may work and get nothing, you are working in contests, you will compete with other designers and even if all the designs are professional, the customer will choose the one he likes best. Here comes the probability of not winning the contest and you will work without getting money.

Even if it doesn't sound well, the more contests you enter, the more chances you have to win them and earn money. The best part is that when you earn a few contest you will be rated and get a badge (bronze, silver, gold and platinum).

When you achieve the Platinum level, you will get constant project and you will be contacted by people, even 99desings will recommend you, as you will be part of the elite designers on their website.

For instance, for a web page, you will charge 599$ as a Bronze designer, 899$ as a Silver designer, 1,599$ as a Gold designer and 2,499$ as a Platinum designer.

You can design a lot more products, not just web pages, you can create book covers, logos, web pages, banners, brochures, app designs, business cards, logos for clothes, any kind of business designs.

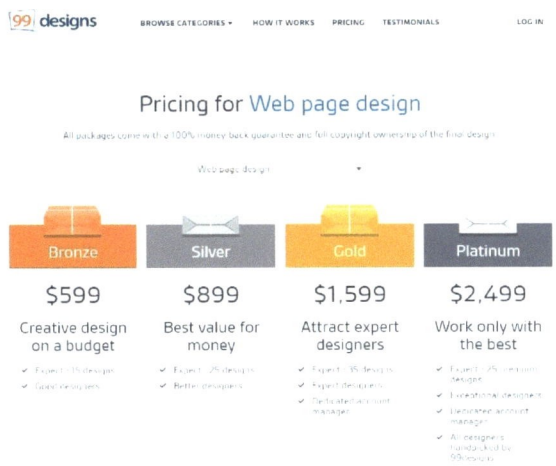

What you need for Web Design?

A laptop / PC, Adobe Photoshop and to study Photoshop (learn from YouTube tutorials, or pay for high quality courses on Udemy for instance). If you never worked in Photoshop, within 6 months you will learn all you need to know in order to make money. In 1 year or less you will make money and you will be able to create new income streams easily. The only thing that matters is if you really want to work and succeed.

Tip: You can make Themes as a passive income, you can work on projects actively and you can even create Udemy courses / YouTube tutorials about how to create themes / projects or eve to create a full Photoshop course in order to make another passive income stream.

# Chapter 8: Work As Virtual Assistant (VA)

This kind of income stream is an active one and it will not bring you thousands of dollars in your pocket but it will provide you with an extra amount of money which you can use to do other things (like Kindle Publishing, you can invest in writing some books and publish them to make even more money) or if you want you can use it as pocket money.

A Virtual Assistant, earns at the beginning 2.5 – 5$ / hour (you can be paid /task though) and you can easily earn 300-400$/ month just by doing this. An advanced, PRO, experienced Virtual Assistant can earn even between 15–30$/hour and notice that if you work 4 hours a day you can earn between 1800 and 3600$ / month as a part time job from your laptop from your home or from wherever you want!

Now what does a Virtual Assistant need to do? You will work for somebody who runs a small business (generally a home business, website, blog etc.) and who doesn't have any time to manage that business. It may also be possible for that person to run other business and again, he needs additional support.

And now let's think logically – what else is simpler, faster and more comfortable than hiring somebody online – you do certain tasks and you get paid by each task or by each hour.

Where can you find VA freelance jobs?

You can search on www.elance.com or www.odesk.com or www.freelancer.com and you will find a lot of jobs from people around the world. The following screenshot is from www.freelancer.com

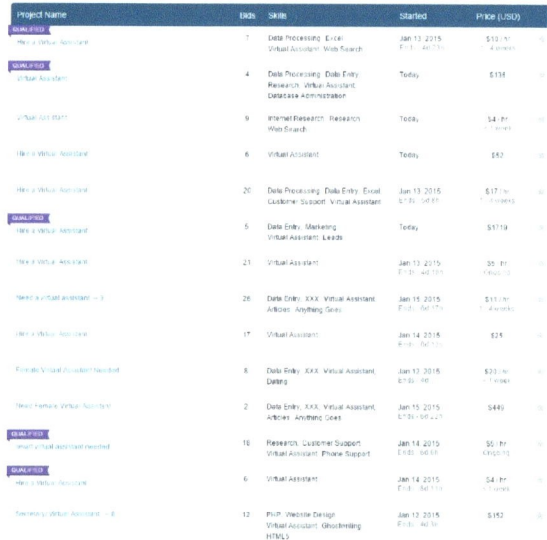

The best part of a VA is that you can see certain things about the company that your boss runs or the small business he runs and you will be able to learn new stuff. With the things you learn and the money you earn you will probably be able to start up your own small business, this is the whole point, to get started in doing something, even when you do not have any money.

The worst part about working as a VA is that there is a lot of competition – anybody can do this so expect all kinds of nations competing for a job like this.

For a beginning, working as a VA to earn a small amount of money in order for you to succeed in other income stream businesses, it's really a good way to start.

# Chapter 9: Work As A Photographer

Don't get mad, I am not telling you to take shots for albums or to schedule studio meetings or to work on a daily basis. What I mean by working as a Photographer is to travel around the world, think of shooting different popular places, take shots in the wild, in different cities. With the photos you take with your DSLR (yes you will need to invest in a DSLR or a professional camera) you will edit them or hire somebody to edit them professionally and you will then sell them online => passive income.

Who buys stock licensed photos?

Most of the big companies which respect themselves are looking for good quality photos to put on their website, projects etc.

We are not allowed to use images from Google which anybody can access and use those photos in international projects or any kinds of projects, it's against the law (copyright). So, the solution is to buy professional stock images from different websites who host stock photos.

You can generally take shots of everything:

- A cup of coffee
- A landscape
- An animal
- A car
- A city or city

- A cityscape
- Anything which inspires you
- Anything original

Those photos you take will need to be edited in Adobe Photoshop or a similar photo editing software and you will upload them on the web. You can buy/sell stock photos on www.shutterstock.com or www.istockphoto.com or www.fotolia.com

These are the main 3 biggest websites which host stock photos, there are others though, but these are the biggest and the most popular.

Prices for stock photos are pretty high and it generally depends on the size of the photo and the type of license that you get. Here's an example photo for the keyword "Business" that I typed. I chose a random result and here it is below:

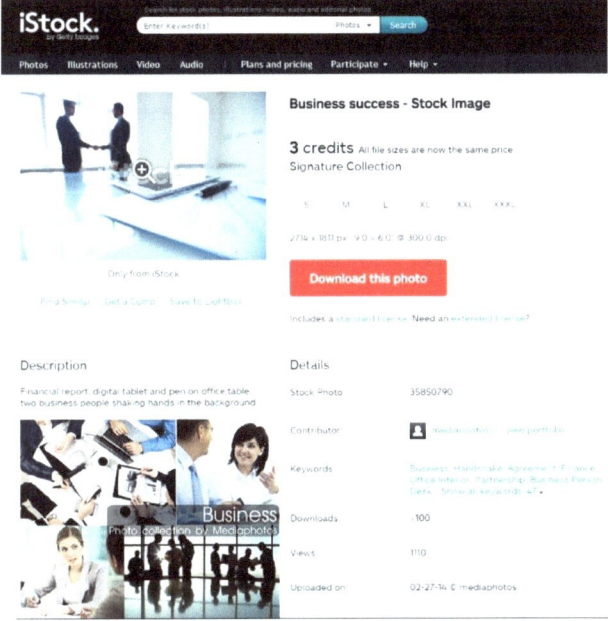

As you may see, there are different sizes, two types of licenses and the price for this photo is 3 credits. Everything is priced in iStockphoto credits which represent a big amount of money. In order to save some money if you need a lot of photos you can make subscriptions and save some cash.

Incredible stock. Flexible pricing.

| Pay per download with credits | | | | Subscribe and save |
|---|---|---|---|---|
| Download the images, vectors and video clips you need with credits - buy more, save more. Your credits never expire at iStock. | | | | Get our best rates on photos, vectors and illustrations. Video and audio clips not included. |
| **3** CREDITS $33 USD | **12** CREDITS $115 USD | **24** CREDITS $220 USD | **36** CREDITS $325 USD | **Essentials Subscription** Millions of everyday images at a ridiculously low price. AS LOW AS **133**$^{25€}$ for 750 images/month (one year plan) |
| 1 CREDIT | | | $12 USD | |
| 6 CREDITS | | | $60 USD | |
| 18 CREDITS | | | $170 USD | **Signature Subscription** |
| 60 CREDITS | | | $520 USD | Every Essentials image plus over 5 million premium images only from iStock |
| 150 CREDITS | | | $1,250 USD | AS LOW AS **266**$^{58€}$ |
| 300 CREDITS | | | $2,400 USD | for 750 images/month (one year plan) |
| Need larger credit packs? Contact us | | | | |

This photo got over 100+ downloads (purchases), so this photo got 300+ credits. As 3 credits are 33$, it means that 100+ downloads generated more than 3300$ for this stock photo, which you can see, it looks really well and professional, but it isn't that hard to make. You are going to pay some fees and commissions for the money you earn, but in any case, you do get some serious money! Imagine if you make 1000 or even more photos like this one, you are going to make a fortune.

You will need a good professional DSLR (1000 – 5000$) and you will need to study the art of photography and attend to some courses though. It isn't that easy, but it generates passive income each month, and you can take shots and edit them from anywhere!

# Chapter 10: Work As A 3D Designer

This is a hard working income stream, but it can be really profitable if you are good at and you make a lot of 3D models. This process is a lot more complex than the others mentioned above, I have presented to you some income streams that don't require any investment or any knowledge. Unfortunately, working as a 3D Artist requires to have a high performance desktop / PC, a lot of work to put in, patience, knowledge and imagination.

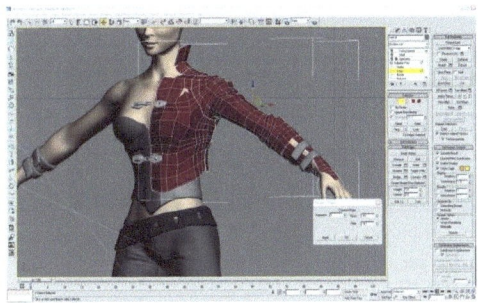

Now let me present you the whole process:

You make a base design (base mesh) in Autodesk 3Ds Max, Autodesk Maya, Cinema 4D or Blender, you export the base mesh into ZBrush or Autodesk Mudbox to enhance some more details and re-export the detailed model in Autodesk Maya or 3Ds Max for rendering.

To design a base mesh takes about 2-3 days or even less if you are an expert, enhancing details can take up to a week and preparing for rendering is also tricky, as you have to play with lights and all the tools from the software.

I am not going to present you all the 3D process because this is just informational, not professional, so I am going to focus on the time to design, the money you can get from doing this and how it's done as a principle.

The whole point is that you make a good 3D model in about 2 weeks and you can get from 50 to 1000$ / purchase. The models that you design can be certificated on www.turbosquid.com as Check Mate Lite or Check Mate PRO and you will get more exposure and a bigger probability to sell your model.

This is an advanced 3D model made and checked in all the software mentioned in the right of the image and there is the certification logo (Check Mate Lite) and the price 699$ for a purchase. This is an expensive, but a very high quality model.

What sells a 3D model? Well there are a lot of factors:

- The number of polygons (the lower, the better, for a certain level of quality)
- The textures
- The rig
- Animations

- The renderings
- The type of model

Let me show you a difference between models which were designed back in 1999 or less and the models that are being designed now. (2013+)

The left model has less than 1000 polygons in total, and the one from the right has more than 50.000 – 100.000 polygons. When there are more polygons, the quality is better, but the Graphics Processor (GPU) needs to be expensive and to deliver a high performance.

What also increases the price of the model a lot is the animations and the rig. To animate (move) a 3D model you will need to create a rig (skeleton of the body) and to put controls.

Now you will probably ask what do people do with this 3D stuff?

Well...the market is wide:

- 3D games for PC
- 3D Games for Xbox/ Play Station
- Commercials
- Movies
- Special Effects

The biggest market comes from 3D games.

Now let's talk about the money process. If you make a model in every two weeks and sell it for 100$ and you will make around 30 models in one year, let's say that you will sell 30-40 units in a month of 100$, you will earn about 4000$. The royalties that Turbosquid offers are from 40 to 80% depending on your sales and much more factors.

The conclusion is that you can earn a lot more than 3000$ / month for example after an year of hard work and then you will be able to passively generate that money each month. The condition is to work hard and to make good quality models. This isn't for everybody, it's for those who like this, who have some imagination and who have the money and patience to invest in themselves. Remember that the software mentioned above are not free and the PC that you will have to buy won't be expensive as well, for big models you need a lot of RAM and a good CPU. A good PC for 3D

Design can exceed 2000$ and you will also need 2 monitors for the best time results.

There are people on www.turbosquid.com who earn a fortune out of 3D models, but they have worked more than 10 years on this process and now they are enjoying the money they earn each month.

This guy from the picture below has 300 quality models, most of them animals and insects, he charges for one model in average about 500$ and he also has collections. This is another profitable thing about 3D models, combine them in collections and sell it for a lower price / model. I think this guy earns more than 100.000$/month just from these models, but it is possible to be a studio or a small company or team. It's not easy to design all of these alone, or maybe, but in 10 years of constant hard work.

# Chapter 11: Make Money From Websites

Creating different types of websites and blogs can bring you a nice passive income, but it depends on how you want to advertise: to use Google AdSense or affiliate links. I should say to use them both as much as possible in order to generate decent sums.

What is Google AdSense?

Google AdSense is a Google service which provides ads on your website and you get paid for them. (pay per click)

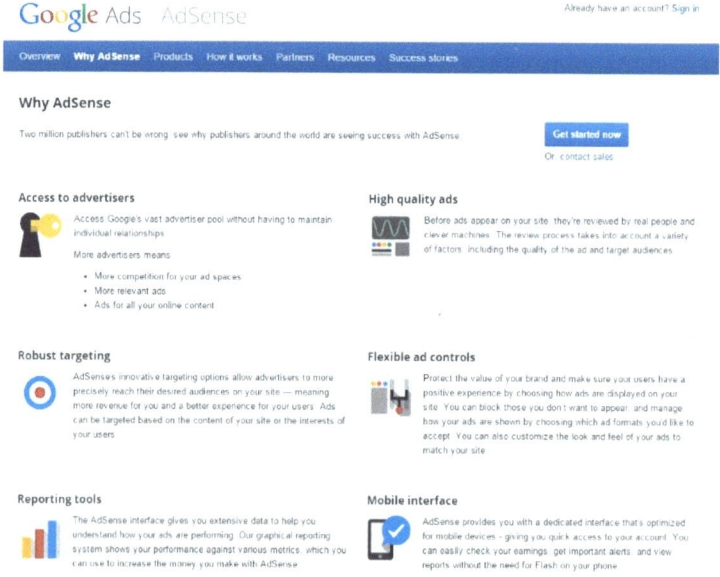

The more traffic you get for your website, the more people will click on those ads  and the more money you will make with your website. It's very profitable when you have a large number of unique visitors each month, otherwise the sums will be really low (especially at the beginning).

Another way to make money on your website is to put affiliate links or to create an aStore – a small store full with Amazon links (affiliate links, for more details about affiliate marketing, please read Chapter 4)

It's indicated to create a website, for example an Automotive website, with car reviews, car news, videos, all kinds of posts etc. and the people that will visit your website everyday will be automotive enthusiasts who are looking for different automotive subjects. Some of them will find interesting a post like "how to drift a car" and you can put along with the article "best drifting tires" and put an affiliate link to buy tires. If people click on that and buy those tires, you will get a commission. The more articles of this kind or news and the more affiliate links and ads you put in your website and the more traffic you get, the more money you will make.

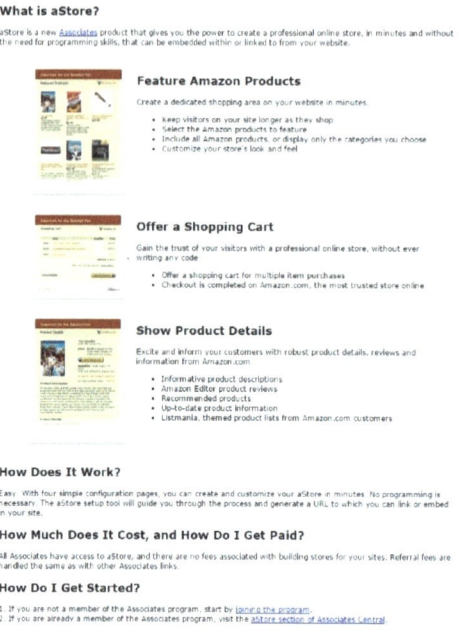

**What is aStore?**

aStore is a new Associates product that gives you the power to create a professional online store, in minutes and without the need for programming skills, that can be embedded within or linked to from your website.

**Feature Amazon Products**

Create a dedicated shopping area on your website in minutes.

- Keep visitors on your site longer as they shop
- Select the Amazon products to feature
- Include all Amazon products, or display only the categories you choose
- Customize your store's look and feel

**Offer a Shopping Cart**

Gain the trust of your visitors with a professional online store, without ever writing any code

- Offer a shopping cart for multiple item purchases
- Checkout is completed on Amazon.com, the most trusted store online

**Show Product Details**

Excite and inform your customers with robust product details, reviews and information from Amazon.com

- Informative product descriptions
- Amazon Editor product reviews
- Recommended products
- Up-to-date product information
- Listmania, themed product lists from Amazon.com customers

**How Does It Work?**

Easy. With four simple configuration pages, you can create and customize your aStore in minutes. No programming is necessary. The aStore setup tool will guide you through the process and generate a URL to which you can link or embed in your site.

**How Much Does It Cost, and How Do I Get Paid?**

All Associates have access to aStore, and there are no fees associated with building stores for your sites. Referral fees are handled the same as with other Associates links.

**How Do I Get Started?**

1. If you are not a member of the Associates program, start by joining the program.
2. If you are already a member of the Associates program, visit the aStore section of Associates Central.

How much does it cost to build a website?

It's relatively cheap, even free for some platforms (for example if you build a free Wordpress blog). In case you want a more premium website you will have to pay for the domain, host and design. It won't charge you more than 500$ if you buy wordpress themes, in case you want a custom design, you can go to www.99designs.com or other places and request a design for your website. This will charge you a lot more, like 3000$ for the design + coding the website.

It's a nice method to generate a passive income, you can hire writers to publish new articles and reviews each day on that website + affiliate links. Google will add automatically its AdSense ads.

And from here, I hope you got the point, you can create 5 websites, on 5 different niches, with Google AdSense, affiliate links, build an aStore within the website, bring traffic and you can generate thousands of dollars each month.

If I'm not wrong, there are blogs and websites which generate over 100,000$/month, but those websites are big, they have more than 5 or 10 years since they were launched and now they are on autopilot and generate passive money.

# Chapter 12: YouTube Videos

One of the most popular ways to make money online passively is to create videos and upload them on YouTube. To generate money from YouTube, you will need:

- A high quality camera (a Full HD 1080p video camera)
- Subscribers
- A lot of videos (high quality videos)

It's generally hard to start a channel from zero and to grow it until the point that you make money, it takes some time until you get a minimum level of popularity, a decent number of videos and a decent number of subscribers. But if you constantly upload videos, people will start to like your work, add you to their favorite list and click on the subscribe button. The principle is simple:

More videos => More subscribers => More views => More money

To upload videos constantly, your channel should be a kind of "series show" like an automotive channel which uploads car reviews, shows, accelerations, thoughts etc. or a comedy show of 5 -10 minutes for each episode. Generally comedy shows are very popular and profitable on YouTube, especially prank series.

For the keyword "Prank" here are the suggestions that YouTube gave me:

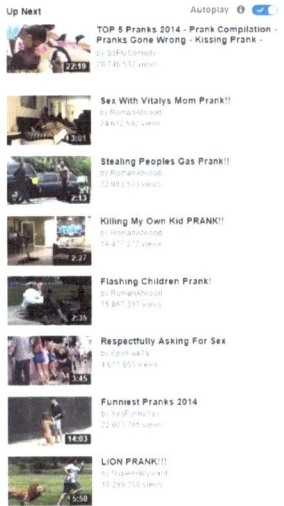

Funny videos are widely searched by people, they want to get entertained and honestly where can you find cool funny videos to watch for free than YouTube?

Vines are also very popular and animals as well. Videos with cats, dogs, weird animals or any kind of weird stuff get views on YouTube.

How you get paid?

When you upload videos on your channel you will be asked if you want to monetize your videos. By saying yes, YouTube will add ads before your video starts (those annoying ads that always show up before each video). Ads are added for local users (local ads for each country) and when somebody clicks on that, you will get paid.

The average sum that you will get is 1 – 5$ / 1000 views. So imagine how much money you will make if you have a series of videos (comedy for example), you make 50 videos in a year and you have at least 100,000 views for each one of them. You can make around 200$/ video and for 50 videos you can make 10,000$ / month (earnings can fluctuate though). Shall I give another example if you have millions of views and at least 100,000 subscribers? I guess not...you can figure out yourself that you can make THOUSANDS of dollars.

The beginning is difficult, but once you get into it, you can make decent money from YouTube. A lot of people made a fortune from YouTube and some people make a living from you this huge platform.

# Chapter 13: Bonus Lesson

Here's is my personal income recipe:

-earn money fast with the least investments and then settle new income streams: start publishing Kindle eBooks and upload them on Amazon, publish a few dozens and generate more than 1000$/month passively (see previous chapters)

-with the money you earn constantly from kindle build a website with affiliate links and market products. Use Google AdSense for additional income. In a couple of months this will also generate you 500-1000$ or even more money passively. (see previous chapters)

-create a digital course about what you have learned, what you do, what you think and upload them on ClickBank and Udemy (see previous chapters)

-find something you like to work actively (web design for example or anything else)

By doing all these things, if you are perseverant and a hard working person, within a couple of years you can earn over 10,000$/month passively or work from overseas, while you are on vacation or travelling. Possibilities are endless! You choose what you want to do, what you want to work, how you want to work and what you want to achieve. It's your choice!

# Conclusion

I want to thank you and congratulate you for downloading the book, you have proved to be interested in making money online and living a better life while others don't even think about it.

By downloading this book proves that you are a wise person who wants a lot more from life. You proved that you want to do something to generate more money and to work harder to improve yourself as a person.

## Congratulations!

I hope this book has been useful to you, even if it's just a short informative one, the purpose of the book was to present to you some proven methods that generate money.

I kindly ask you to leave an honest review when you have the time, share with me what thoughts you have, either if there are bad or good, it will help me improve my books and myself as a person as well.

Kindest Regards,

Frank J. Miller

www.ingramcontent.com/pod-product-compliance
Lightning Source LLC
Chambersburg PA
CBHW040924180526
45159CB00002BA/605